SILHOUETTES OF SOLITUDE

THE UNSEEN INK OF EMOTIONS

NITISH KUMAR R K

Made with ♥ on the Notion Press Platform
www.notionpress.com

Dedicated to,

My Parents, Friends and specially to all the readers and upcoming writers.

Contents

Contents

Preface

"Poetry is when an emotion has found its thought and the thought has found words." – Robert Frost

This book contains a collection of poems written by a mere student, myself, now carrying the title of 'Poet', pursuing Masters in English Language and Literature. As a literature lover, I cherish poetry but had no idea that I would be reciting poems of my own. My poems are complexly built and kindle emotions that are often left unchecked by crowds. They deal with different aspects of life that people may overlook in their daily lives. Therefore, they require special attention to uncover the treasures that readers seek. The themes are well connected to the lives of each individual and can resonate with all of my beloved readers. The title of my book has been meticulously chosen and is associated with solitude, which is a powerful state that allows us to realize many things we often miss. It also reflects my journey in reciting my poetry. This is my first book and I believe it serves as proof for everyone out there that anyone can be a literary artist like me. I hope you all will enjoy my work.

Acknowledgements

I owe a great deal of debt to my parents who have always supported me in this work. Everyone needs and has an inspiration and in the same way, my inspiration to write this work is Professor Samuel Rufus. He was the person who ignited the spark within me with his supportive and optimistic spirit. I extend my sincere gratitude to all my Professors of the department of English. Also I am obliged to two of my bestproofreaders, Veena J and Ann Mariya T, for their splendid work and special thanks to Abraham and Dhanush Kumar for assisting me all through the process. I am thankful for all the above-mentioned people for helping me with my publication and without them, it would have been very difficult task for me.

Personal details:

PROFESSOR SAMUEL RUFUS

(rufus@mcc.edu.in)

VEENA J

(vv6540860@gmail.com/+919361886645)

ANN MARIYA T

(annzmichael03@gmail.com/+917306643721)

1. A Man in the Woods

Upon the woods, there comes a Man
The he-man of the wild and wildings!
Remigrating from the war of a decade,
With a valiance and nobility so expounding.
He wanders in search of a flower
That has sprouted for a quarter- century.
The bush land looks newfound to him,
Becoming obscured to the dim.
Partly in love, Partly in daze
He perceives a bitty sound of an anklet.
In delirium is his heart and soul,
Making him steer through the flow,
Usurped to the scent of a lassy jasmine,
Of two eyes, ears and dimples,
Forming the image of a young maid,
Cast out with sultry stems.
Too gaudy she is to him,
Her glance being an heavenly shower,
For she is my lover whilst the shady bower..

2. The Almighty

Am I alone? No, not at all. Oh Almighty, you lift me up.
I don't fear backstabbers, as a shield protects my back.
There is a mighty sword lying before me to vanquish my foes.
He hides me in His cocoon, surrounding me, preparing me for a tough battle.
Not only does He surround me, but He also resides in my inner shrine.
Blessed are those who take Him into their hearts,
The liberator of our sins and provider of ecstasies.
Is there anything more you could offer us?
Is there anything I should fear?
Is there anyone who could oppose me in your presence?
How can I satisfy your desires with these feeble mortal hands?
Tell me, Oh Almighty.

3. Oh My Mother!!

Oh, my Mother! You are our refuge,
You are a bliss for many downhearted people.
You are a reliable muse for many pen-holders.
You are the mother of all creations,
A mother of all who remains unbigoted towards her infants.
You provide us with comforts and hold us among many plights,
Yet, the desires of your children exploits you.
They are onto power and pride,
And wrack you for your selfless love.
Your breath has become distorted,
Your tears have been dried up,
Your strands of hair are being plucked.
But you continue pouring your selfless love,
And they still run on ravaging you.
What do we deserve for your profound love?
Tell me mother. Oh, my mother!!

4. A Dad's Steadfast Aura

The man who smiles at my delight
And feels misery while I am in it.
The moment I meet him, his heart beats,
Beats only with joy, the joy of my sight.
The conflicts he faces are nowhere,
As they are left behind for love.
His love extends like the ocean, that can engulf me,
But he, like Poseidon, won't allow me to.
We look alike but were born in distant times,
Even the mighty time couldn't separate us,
Since we are the conjoined twins of the time.
I am the Sun to him and he constantly orbits around me,
Guarding me from all evil eyes,
From dawn until dusk.

5. To the Sister of Mine

To the sister of mine,
Who stayed beside me for years.
I remember well the giggles we had,
The thoughts we shared and struggles we faced.
Life drove us into many plights,
And our tireless fights comes to my mind.
Looking back, now it makes me laugh
After all, it couldn't break our bond,
The bond, ordained by God.
I wish we had shared the same womb
To the sister of mine, to whom I write this.

6. "Folks Augment-Your Lens"

The earthlings vary, as do their lenses.
At every moment, each wears a kind of lens
To catch a glimpse of distinct phases in their lives.
This glimpse remains unchanged through time,
From the rise of mankind till the present.
Is the lens worn only to see what we see?
Do they not show you something?
Yes, mine does.
It holds worldly power, moulding life to its needs,
The ability to turn illusions into facts,
To swap the places of Zion and Sheol.
But many lack the potency to wear them.

7. That's how he is

I walk through the road, returning after heavy duty.
The path is teeming with extreme heat.
With each step, sweat flows from my tip to toe.
My eyes search for the white gateway that lies ahead.
I open it with ecstasy and my heart dances in delight.
Now, I finally reach my destination not to rest,
But to gaze at someone who resemble my shadow.
He escorts me wherever I go, and now I finally meet him.
The moment he noticed my return, his legs took off in a quick run,
Like a Pegasus, gliding across the surface to embrace me.

8. Our Nostalgic New Comer

Mid-afternoon, it was resolved to go
Along with my pops and brother.
We drove through the extreme heat,
Quite afar to a peculiar spot,
Where he had been held captive for a while,
Mingled within the pack of the same of his race.
Frightened, was my psyche to barely touch them,
Suddenly one among them leaped out to flee,
Trying to mount on my limbs yet could not.
Now given the choice to pick the odd one,
Each one seemed charming to my eyes
But life yielded only one for me,
Whilst my arms unrestrained picked him up
The only one I yielded to.
We took him in a crate to his new abode,
Yelling, he was to the power of Helios,
Throughout the places, he was heard.
At last, we reached our resting place with him,
Being invited to his new relations,
That either he welcomed or we welcomed him.

9. Blessed Am I…

Blessed are those who draw their breath in poverty.
Blessed are those who endure their life in sickness.
Blessed are those who live and bleed for virtues.
Blessed are those who taste doleful deaths.
Blessed are those who face eternal pains.
Blessed are those who paddle in their tears.
Blessed are those who are blind to deliriums.
Blessed are those who are befriended by isolation.
Blessed are those who are deserted by their soulmates.
For they are blessed with a deific destiny,
To rest in the laps and kiss the cheek of the Almighty.

10. Why is the nature teaching me life?

The reptile has lost his tail,
His tail has been minced up,
Minced up by the laws of nature,
Nature which has been his mother.
Mother have her own reason, doesn't she?
Doesn't she know the creed of life?
Life begins with new cuts,
Cuts that people resist within them
Within them couldn't realise that it regrows,
Regrows into a better new tail,
Tail cast into a new puzzle,
Puzzled by impostors afore.
Some tails can bring hefty downs
That can be eluded for life's crowns.

11. Visit to Paralia

Beaches has been a fair place for many,
That's worth more just a penny,
Now that I dropped my niches,
To free my mind from its hitches,
Sat on the brink shore of the surfs,
Which has been for them as turfs.
Pursuing tirelessly in search of revelation,
Only to find life ceasing in the same notion.
Naive of the life present in this spot,
Where both life and loss have been so hot.
Snails in shoreline come gliding,
Being Inclined to the shell wrapping,
Making a fast procession to skip the tides,
Depicting the alike reality of ours,
Changing for them in the time of hours.
Then comes the end to their quest,
The tides that put them to the eternal rest.
This is also the life for those who run with thirst
Getting dragged into their tombs of dusk,
Such is the life to all the parties.

12. "The Shades of War"

The country is illuminated with an emerald green painting,
In which the land is ravaged in the name of warfare.
Men in wave-green patterns move around the field;
Now everything is turned into brown shades.
They depict the turning of Time;
The time that ruins existence and survival
There they hold weapons and artillery
That massacre mankind over decades.
On the brown, there are splashes of blood
Making the art puzzled with excess colors,
Unable to portray its concrete face.

13. A Glance for my Inner Tot

There is a child budding inside for ages,
Not aged as me but with the clock!
His smile can spread joy across the heavens,
But his fault caught in woes,
By the arrows pulled at my side.
It is him who gets stung by them,
And for his past left him bruised
Full of coughs, sneezes and cries
Making him bedridden day in and day out.
Solacing him required a great labor
Yet those life spikes left an eternal wound,
Remembering the time of his nursing.
Sets my eyes with pebbles of tears,
For now I age in time and He in defiance; A huge resistance;
As his pappa and mamma 'I' call him 'My beloved inner child'.

14. The Anchor for my Malaise

The storm dances outside while my heart dances in distress.
Sitting in the nook of a room walled in darkness,
I feel flustered and dejected, with my hands and legs shivering
A ray of light passes through the lunette flashing,
But still, there isn't a blaze within me
My heart, in isolation, aches and pleads for aid;
All alone, there lies a mirror in front,
A shadow leaps from it, resembling me.
My eyes stuck on, I see a bougie wielded in its hand,
Seducing my heart to serenity and finally nearing me
It said "I will be your anchor in the storm".

15. Maxims of a True heart

Belief in you can bring you to a
Destination;
Belief in others can take you to a
death station.
Love is like a dove that flies away
when you stop feeding it anymore.
Broken minds need logging off not
shutdowns.
Truth is a decayed tooth for
mouth-liars
For these are the maxims of the true heart
In The world where lies are the only art.

Quote time

'Move on is undone until one heals their disgust feels..'

~NITISH KUMAR R K

16. HER - An honest expression of reminiscence

Is it her?
Is it her who came into my life?
Is it her who bantered with me?
Is it her who tended to me despite being a toddler herself?
Is it her with whom I bonded with?
Is it her who had an untainted soul?
Is it her, or me, who left...?

17. Muse - My Divine Specter

Who was that? The one who dove; into the dome
Where my thoughts and sensations wander.
I hear a tender voice amongst the lingering memoirs - A woman's voice
Her articulation seemed so intact like a chord,
Giving the same bliss as a specter's voice
She talks in melody and her words flowed,
Throughout my body inflaming my blood
The hands and fingers once ceased to work,
Began composing with the voice of my divine specter.

18. Wanna be Rich?

Richness conducts the globe to revolve,
Also did drove us to evolve.
Subsist within our sense,
But is still lost among the dense.
Keen have they become to those radiant
That can be theirs or gradient
Centuries passed for us to pitch,
Into the quarter that makes us rich
To those rich, embrace these:
Rich are those who live by currency
Richer are those who live by devotion
Riches are those who live by sense
Richest are those who live in the glee of other species.

19. Prolonged Seclusion

I see mankind rushing for shekels
Spirits derided by lustrous allure.
The globe twirls for futilities,
The futilities that roused unaptly as time ran on,
Until the Black Death colonized us.
This time, doughs had not been looted
Rather on the lives that had existed,
Airless it has been for a quadrennial,
Countless coffins stacked on one another,
Hospices turned into boneyards.
There were no folks to weep
Is this a penance from the Elysium?
Later came the blessed martyrs for the need,
Sent to liberate the striving souls.
They came, freed and left
But these minds disagrees to it,
They eat, sleep and hoard...

20. Summon or Conjure? -The Curse I wish for

Trampling along the trails, my eyes wandering,
While cogitations constantly nag at me
Am I dwelling on the hills of Tartarus?
My head feels too heavy to bear
"Adieu, Adieu" tells my insights
This boulder seems to weigh a ton
I fail in forging the boulder ahead,
Now my feet are thrown off balance, losing their direction
Where am I being led?
Afore lies an enticing orchard,
Budding with reddish-pink florals, resembling an archangel.
The very intimidating archangel to me.
Did she summon me? Had she before? I wish she had.
So close we are that her fragrance fills my airsacs
Shinier her tiara is, in a blink I see it on top
On my head, fitted by her blazing arms.
In an instant, I am laid down on the terrene,
Now with the countenance of a cloudless sky
As I woke up, she is no longer there,
But engraved in my wairua forever...

21. Behind every veils

People often put on masks these days,
To hide their emotions and motives.
The real one is concealed behind different masks,
With feelings left behind.
Considering the colossal use of masks,
The countenance shown before us cannot be justified.
Now there is a bafflement within ourselves
As to which masks to wear before each person;
these mask that fiddles with our reality,
persuading us into falseness and deception,
Producing a set of actors who distort their own reality.

22. The Unstoppable Grit

The runners are ready and tightened.
Now I come to the shore, where the sun glazes upon me.
The track is full of sand, and the air scents salty.
Beyond lies my destination, far away.
It seemed harsh, but my mind told, "Do it."
My legs took off, leaving behind every regret.
On my journey, there were peaks and valleys,
But they couldn't shake off my persistence.
After reaching halfway, the struggle became more challenging.
My legs trembling, and my eyes glancing back at the path.
Turning my head forward 'against my will' I could see my destination getting closer.
My lungs were about to explode, and I gasped for more breath.
To continue the course and finally achieve it.

23. Silent Seekers

Yo Introverts! I know how acute silence is..
I often see you guys lonely with your own time,
As strangers to your inner selves,
Concealed from the outer world's sublime,
And to the joy and chitchats you deserve.
It is not that I disturb your quietude,
But always remember, There is a heart inside,
which throbs to have delight amidst the silence....

24. The feeling of being loved

To people in love,
Love is to love and to be loved,
To trust and to be trusted,
To turn inward and to be turned inward,
To sway and to be swayed,
To battle and to be battled,
To guard and to be guarded,
To amuse and to be amused,
To give and to be given,
To favour and to be favoured,
To acquire and to be acquired.
For each, it is a necessity and a need,
Yet the needy is stressed to unlove their love,
When their faith for love is runs low.

25. A Tribute to the Legend – William Shakespeare

One sleeps while the other arises
The Sun and Moon plays seesaw seizing the turf,
It seems both of their reigns are tough.
Perching on an attic to ponder,
Where My minds wander;
About a legend,
Who has now tuned us to be intend.
who seemed an upstart crow to one,
while the others charge him as slow-witted none.
For dusting Greek and latin with build gramm;
Before his name, was he tagged the mimicker,
Scathed on the terrain of briers was his life.
But my notion of him vacillates from everyone.
Piles of stars lie on the dark carpet,
Summoning the bards stacked in my memory;
for each star held one's face:
John Donne, Spenser, Sir Wyatt, Sackville and Sidney.
But where is Shakespeare among them?

My eyes couldn't locate him or his lyrics,
Reviewing again but no blot of him is spotted.
Sombre, it was, to think of the others,
But turned towards the moon that healed my heart-sick,
'Cause of his presence in the cosmic white orb,
which gleams brighter than the tiny ones.
The oldest of the older, the eldest of the elders,
His eternity is the glint to those luminous stars of his age,
lit up by his deistic ray, the Shakespearean ray...

26. Once a boon to doom

Diffused into the illusion of reality:
Everybody got their own compatriots
That inheres to no existing breeds,
The breeds that have seized the human race,
Which has been battling to not get ruled anon.
Alas had been fooled by mere touch-screens,
With bright light on their faces confined too long,
Fetching the whole mankind to annihilation.
Excluded from the society now they are,
Wedged with their own bought compatriots.
The sense of alienation now in the progress,
Making the living bodies as breathing corpses,
Guiding our mortal souls immorally.

27. Ponder your Birther's pain

Shame, shame, Truly shame!
Shame it is to surrender to death isn't it?
Before your elders and grannies..?
Think you are born into this world
By defeating doom by the womb.
And your mamma battled the army of the dead
To grab you by your small tenderly paws,
But now you are ready to give your soul to him..?
For the miseries and punies to sustain,
Not only killing the life of yours,
But betray the blood of your birther,
The blood she blew to slaughter the knights of death.

28. Silent screams and Violent riots

The days of this century are lavishly lecherous,
And mankind has tended to become most barbarous.
Eyeing for some high-tech upgrades,
Decided to desert their diabolic ways.
For their breath of defilement is immense,
Making them vermin beyond human sense.
Futile it is to offer any cureness,
That no riots can halt this lewdness.
No cannons (or) codes can transit this ill's might,
Until people set themselves to every victim's plight.

29. "Poem Reepers"

To those who appeal them as poets,
Also to be reputed as mindful tillers,
Are served with an ideal plot to plow,
Where stillness becomes (their) plough,
And theme being their only seed,
Like a good subject to the Master-
Is to yield a Firm Foetus in the field.
Idioms as the worms are the esse
Thence flicked into those croplands
To enrich the lushness of the plot.
As the tilling-poet ceases in action,
Its the audience to foster this growing child
By raining on him with PRAISES!!
Only that, Can make him speak the honor of its creator
That He is the one who farmed him, and yielded..

30. Walk with me to Poetica

Dear readers,
I know you are fret by this weary life,
But come with me through these lines into a utopian world
With a pleasant sky and many scented flowers,
Surrounded by people of smiles and ecstacies.
Ages lead people away from death,
With illnesses buried from the mankind forever.
No search for jobs is needed here
And employees to fear fatigue and dismissals.
Here, the currencies does not matter,
The rate race being pushed to lose,
As everything here are in abundance,
Where people can pass through any of their lifespan
To the Age of 10 or 20s, 45 or 60s
This whole world is distilled from the scums,
As are the emotions of each ones.
In the distance you can see the God's hill
Where people are free to sit and chat with him as their will.

Quote time

'Each have their own shrine deep down
But it is the worship that assorts the pure soul from the human foul..'

~NITISH KUMAR R K

Author's Bio

Nitish Kumar R K is a dedicated and aspiring young writer currently pursuing his postgraduate degree in English language and literature at Madras Christian College. He has been actively involved in writing poetry, blogs and quotes. His poetry style is tremendous with a complex meaning to it. This poetry book is a complete mix of themes where one could easily empathize and it also contains a few poems that reflect his perception of this artistic world. He is very enthusiastic to share his first book of poetry with a wider audience and prove himself as an exemplary poet to the world.

P.S: This book provides a wonderful experience in terms of themes, complexity, and vocabulary. Let's enjoy and encourage him.

www.ingramcontent.com/pod-product-compliance
Lightning Source LLC
LaVergne TN
LVHW041256150826
845673LV00008B/2620

* 9 7 9 8 8 9 6 3 2 8 6 9 8 *